"Using the riches o
daily prompts to
for our kids. This
yourself and give
community. I high

Megan Hill, Author, *Praying Together*;
mother of three

"I can easily fall into a rut when praying for my children. I am so thankful, therefore, for this fresh, new book. The layout is clear, the framing is biblical, the prayer prompts are brief, and the value—for us, for our kids, and for the glory of Christ—is eternal."

Matt Smethurst, Managing Editor,
The Gospel Coalition; Author,
1–2 Thessalonians: A 12-Week Study

"What a biblical and handy tool Melissa has given us to use as we pray for our children! I look forward to giving this resource to parents and grandparents in our church and family."

Christine Hoover, Author, *Messy Beautiful Friendship* and *Searching for Spring*

"This book is a great resource to encourage parents and the entire church family to pray specifically and thoughtfully for the children in their care."

Steven Condy, Child Evangelism Fellowship

"This book is a gift to the church. This guide has helped my wife and me, as new parents, pray for more aspects of our son's life."

Phillip Holmes, Director of Communications and Marketing, Reformed Theological Seminary

"This book should be given to every parent in the church—and every children's-ministry leader too—so that they can pray without ceasing for the children in our congregations."

Ruth Bromley, Children's Development Officer,
Presbyterian Church of Ireland

"In an age of helicopter parenting, it's easy for us parents to think that our children's future rests in our hands. Melissa Kruger gives us the practical steps we need to take all we can't control to the One whose goodness reigns supreme. Because in the end, the very best thing we parents can do with our hands is fold them... in prayer."

Hannah Anderson, Author, *All That's Good*;
mother of three

"In *5 Things to Pray for Your Kids*, Melissa Kruger takes us to Scripture to pray God's word through the seasons of parenting life. What greater gift and model can we offer our children than to be prayerful parents, committing ourselves and our children to God's grace?"

Ivan Mesa, Books Editor, The Gospel Coalition

"Melissa Kruger delivers an accessible prayer primer targeted at the intention and aim of every parent. Her prayers strike a keen balance between the practical and theological. This book casts our eyes and heart upward to God, our only hope for raising kids who live in light of eternity."

Karen Hodge, Coordinator for Women's Ministry,
Presbyterian Church in America

THINGS TO
PRAY
5
FOR YOUR
KIDS

MELISSA B. KRUGER

thegoodbook
COMPANY

5 things to pray for your kids
Prayers that change things for the next generation
© Melissa Kruger, 2019. Reprinted 2019 (twice).
Series Editor: Carl Laferton

Published by:
The Good Book Company

thegoodbook.com | www.thegoodbook.co.uk
thegoodbook.com.au | thegoodbook.co.nz | thegoodbook.co.in

Unless indicated, all Scripture references are taken from the Holy
Bible, New International Version. Copyright © 2011 Biblica, Inc.TM
Used by permission.

ISBN: 9781784982928 | Printed in Denmark

Design by André Parker

CONTENTS

PRAYING THAT I WILL...

PRAYING WHEN MY CHILD IS...

INTRODUCTION

BY EMMA KRUGER

My mom once said that learning to pray was like learning another language. If you grew up with parents who prayed regularly in the home, it would feel natural—like a native language you'd spoken since birth. But if you waited, it became harder to learn. It wasn't that you couldn't learn to pray, but it might take more time for it to feel natural.

That's why I'm so grateful to have grown up with prayerful parents. From a young age, I was taught what prayer was and how to do it. I prayed with others at church, school, meals, and family devotions. It was always just a part of who I was and felt like a normal part of life. Looking back on the past seventeen years of learning and growing in prayer, I realize what an impact my parents praying for me and with me have had.

My parents didn't give me a class to teach me how to pray. There was no instruction manual, video, or lecture. I simply learned by watching them pray each and every day. Every evening, sitting by my bed, my dad would read a Bible story and pray with my siblings and me. Every morning I would come downstairs for school and see my mom finishing up her quiet time as she wrote out her prayers to the Lord. I knew that, among other things, she had been praying for me— asking God to grow my knowledge and love of Christ. And in a way, God used my mom's prayers to answer my mom's prayers: it was through seeing her alone with the Lord every morning that I began to prioritize this same sort of time for myself and understand the importance of it.

My parents' example also taught me what to look for in Christian community. Prayer is an essential part of their friendships, and I've sought out this same type of community with my high-school friends. By seeing my parents pray for those who are suffering, I began to understand the importance of the church family in the intense trials of life. Now, as I prepare to leave home for college, I'm looking for this same com- munity of prayer and care for one another that my parents have shown me.

Prayer is a vital part of walking with God. I've seen the way it strengthens faith. My parents have faithfully encouraged me in it. I'll forever be thankful for the ways in which they've taught me and supported me in prayer, showing me what it means to have a personal relationship with our Lord Jesus Christ.

Emma Kruger
Melissa's daughter

HOW TO USE THIS GUIDE

This guide will help you to pray for children in 21 different areas and situations—be that your own child, or (with a little adaptation) your grandchild, godchild, or a family at church. There are five different things to pray for each of the 21 areas, so you can use this book in a variety of ways.

➤ *You can pray through a set of "five things" each day, over the course of three weeks, and then start again.*

➤ *You can take one of the prayer themes for the week and pray one point every day from Monday to Friday.*

➤ *Or you can dip in and out of it, as and when you want and need to pray for a particular aspect of family life.*

➤ *There's also a space on each page for you to write in the names of specific situations, concerns, or children that you intend to remember in prayer.*

Each prayer suggestion is based on a passage of the Bible, so you can be confident as you use this guide that you are praying great prayers—prayers that God wants you to pray, because they're based on his word.

PRAYING THAT GOD WILL...

SAVE MY
CHILD

EPHESIANS 2 v 8-10

PRAYER POINTS:

_____

_____

_____

_____

Father, I pray that you would hear my prayers and do what only your Spirit can do. Cause my child to…

BE SAVED BY GRACE

"For it is by grace you have been saved" (v 8).

It's sometimes tempting to believe that if we can be perfect parents, then our children will grow into perfect Christians. However, it's good to remember that our children aren't saved by "perfect parenting" but by God's amazing grace. Pray daily that God will save your child.

BE GIVEN THE GIFT OF FAITH

"… through faith—and this is not from yourselves, it is the gift of God" (v 8).

Praise God that he offers the free gift of salvation by grace alone, through faith alone! While it can be difficult for children to believe in what they cannot see, faith allows them to gain spiritual vision and understanding. Pray that your child will have faith from a young age and believe the message of the gospel.

BOAST IN CHRIST ALONE

"… not by works, so that no one can boast"
(v 9).

Our children love to show us what they've accomplished. They proudly paint pictures or give us positive reports of their test scores. It can be difficult for them to believe salvation is not based on their works or performance. Pray that your child will clearly understand the radical gospel message and boast in Christ alone.

 GROW TO BE LIKE JESUS

"For we are God's handiwork, created in
Christ Jesus" (v 10).

We often look at our children, noticing how they reflect us. However, they are created to reflect Jesus more than anyone else. Pray that as your child grows, they would increasingly shine Jesus to the watching world.

 PREPARE FOR GOOD WORKS

"… to do good works, which God prepared
in advance for us to do" (v 10).

James tells us that "faith by itself, if it is not accompanied by action, is dead" (James 2 v 17). Pray that your child's faith would overflow in good works that glorify God. Ask God to give you opportunities to see their faith in action as they clean up after dinner, respond kindly to a sibling, or pray for a friend in need.

5 THINGS TO PRAY

PRAYING THAT GOD WILL...

FILL MY CHILD WITH SPIRITUAL FRUIT

GALATIANS 5 v 22-23

PRAYER POINTS:

_____

_____

_____

_____

_____

Father, I pray that your Spirit will bear fruit in my child…

 LOVE

"But the fruit of the Spirit is love" (v 22).

Praise God that by his Spirit he gives us a new heart that bears good fruit. Our hope as parents is that our love for our children reflects God's great love for them. Pray that as they experience the love of God, they would love others—that they would share their toys, comfort those who are hurting, and look out for others who may be lonely.

 JOY AND PEACE

"… joy, peace" (v 22).

Jesus told his disciples, "In this world you will have trouble" (John 16 v 33). He also told them that he would be the source of their joy and peace in the midst of their trials. Pray that the Lord will give your child joy in all circumstances and peace that transcends understanding.

FORBEARANCE AND KINDNESS

"… forbearance, kindness" (v 22).

Being part of any family requires forbearance and kindness. Living in close quarters means we can easily annoy one another. Pray that your children will patiently bear with one another in love, remembering that they so often need to be shown patience and kindness as well.

GOODNESS AND FAITHFULNESS

"… goodness, faithfulness" (v 22).

Praise God that he is the author of all that is good and he is faithful in all he does. Our children have many moments before them each day when they will choose whether to listen to God's ways or go their own way. Today, pray that your child will follow God's word and faithfully do what is good.

GENTLENESS AND SELF-CONTROL

"… gentleness and self-control" (v 23).

Self-control paired with gentleness is something we all hope to see in our children. Consider today where your child is struggling with self-control. Perhaps they are having a difficult time controlling their temper, limiting their screen time, or following your directions. Pray the Lord will give them both self-control to do what is right and gentleness in their attitude as they obey.

PRAYING THAT GOD WILL...

WATCH OVER MY CHILD

PSALM 121

PRAYER POINTS:

_____

_____

_____

_____

Father, I pray that you will help my child by...

 ENCOURAGING ME

> *"I lift up my eyes to the mountains—where does my help come from? My help comes from the LORD" (v 1).*

Being a parent is a wonderful gift, but it is also difficult. There's no owner's manual to guide us in all the choices we face each day. Praise God that we can turn to him for the help we need! Pray that he will guide your steps and lead you as you parent today.

 WATCHING OVER THEM

> *"He who watches over you will not slumber; indeed, he who watches over Israel will neither slumber nor sleep" (v 3-4).*

As parents, we are limited. Even with modern technology, we can't watch our children at every moment (although we certainly try!). Thank God that he is always watching over them, and that he never slumbers or sleeps. Pray that your child will know God is with them, no matter where they go or what they face.

PROVIDING REFRESHMENT

> *"The LORD is your shade at your right hand;*
> *the sun will not harm you by day, nor the*
> *moon by night" (v 5-6).*

We all need a place of refuge. The world can be difficult and lonely. Pray that when life is hard for your child—when they experience a broken heart, a difficult illness, or a painful consequence—they will turn to the Lord and find comfort in him.

 ## KEEPING THEM FROM HARM

> *"The LORD will keep you from all harm—he*
> *will watch over your life" (v 7).*

While we want to keep our children safe, we know we are often powerless to protect them from skinned knees, harmful gossip, and their own mistakes. Pray that the Lord will use the trials they endure to draw them closer to himself, and that he will keep them from all that he sees is harmful.

 ## PROTECTING THEIR FUTURE

> *"The LORD will watch over your coming and*
> *going both now and forevermore" (v 8).*

Our children make choices each day. As they grow, these choices increase in significance. Pray that the Lord would guide your child in the future as they choose what to study, which church to be part of, who to marry, or what job to pursue.

PRAYING THAT MY CHILD WILL...

HAVE CONFIDENCE IN JESUS

HEBREWS 10 v 22-25

PRAYER POINTS:

_____

_____

_____

_____

Father, I pray that my child will trust in Jesus and by faith...

 DRAW NEAR

> *"Let us draw near to God with a sincere heart and with the full assurance that faith brings" (v 22).*

Praise God that by the blood of Jesus we have access to a new and living way into God's awesome presence (v 19-20). Jesus paved the way, so we can walk in fellowship with God. Pray that your child will draw near to God today, thinking about him and seeking him with a sincere heart.

 HOLD FAST

> *"Let us hold unswervingly to the hope we profess, for he who promised is faithful" (v 23).*

It's tempting to run after false gods and worldly wisdom. Ask God to help your child hold fast to the truths of the gospel without wavering. Pray that he would work in their lives in such a way that they cannot remember a day when they didn't know him.

CONSIDER OTHERS

*"Let us consider how we may spur one
another on toward love and good deeds"
(v 24).*

Thankfully, one of the gifts God gives us is community with other believers. Pray that your child will have godly mentors that spur them on in faith, love, and good works. As you pray for your child, consider: how can you encourage them to love others and do good works today?

 MEET TOGETHER

*"... not giving up meeting together, as
some are in the habit of doing" (v 25).*

If they're going to keep going in Christ, our children need the church. Pray that when they grow up, the Lord will place them in churches where the word is preached and the gospel is proclaimed. Ask God to grow in your child a deep love for the church that starts now and lasts throughout their life.

 LOOK FORWARD

*"... and all the more as you see the Day
approaching" (v 25).*

Our children are young, but time is short. Ask God to give them the right perspective on eternity. Pray they would look forward to Christ's return with confidence, knowing they will be found righteous in him; and with urgency, seeking to make the best use of the time.

PRAYING THAT MY CHILD WILL...

EXPERIENCE GOD'S GREATNESS

ISAIAH 40 v 28-31

PRAYER POINTS:

_____

_____

_____

_____

*Father, please help my child to know you and worship
you as…*

 ## CREATOR

> *"Do you not know? Have you not heard?
> The LORD is … the Creator of the ends of
> the earth" (v 28).*

God is the Creator of the ends of the earth, including
all the little corners of your neighborhood that your
family loves. At the same time, our lives have special
meaning because we're created in the image of God.
Praise God for this world he created and for the way
he uniquely created your child. Pray your child will
know God and worship him as Creator and Lord of all.

 ## EVERLASTING

> *"The LORD is the everlasting God" (v 28).*

God is eternal. He has no beginning and no end.
While all other leaders' reigns will come to an end,
God reigns forever and ever. Pray that your child will
know Jesus and worship him as King, for all eternity.

ALL-KNOWING

"He will not grow tired or weary, and his understanding no one can fathom" (v 28).

God knows all things, and the depths of his understanding no one can fathom. While God is incomprehensible, he *is* knowable. Praise God that he reveals truth about himself in the Bible. Pray that your child would seek to know God through his word and look to God as the source of knowledge, wisdom, and understanding.

 **ALL-POWERFUL**

"He gives strength to the weary and increases the power of the weak" (v 29).

Our children are limited. But they long to be in charge and claim, "I do it myself!" However, they quickly run out of energy and easily become tired and frustrated. Thankfully, God is never tired or weary. Pray your child would acknowledge their own weakness and look to God for strength. Pray that the Spirit would empower your child to live in a way that glorifies God.

 ALL-SUFFICIENT

"Those who hope in the LORD will renew their strength" (v 31).

God promises to sustain us: "They will soar on wings like eagles; they will run and not grow weary, they will walk and not be faint" (v 31). Ask God to renew your strength as you faithfully parent today.

PRAYING THAT MY CHILD WILL...

DELIGHT IN GOD'S WORD

PSALM 19 v 7-12

PRAYER POINTS:

Father, I pray that your word will give my child...

 REFRESHMENT

> *"The law of the LORD is perfect, refreshing the soul" (v 7).*

Family life is fast-paced—even for the youngest members. While we cannot know all that our children experience, we do know they have struggles. Whatever they face, God's word is a source of refreshment. Pray that your child will love God's word, and that it will revive their soul as they journey throughout different seasons and circumstances.

 JOY

> *"The precepts of the LORD are right, giving joy to the heart" (v 8).*

Praise God that his word is able to give us delight— it's more desirable than gold and "sweeter ... than honey" (v 10). Ask God to give your child joy as they read Scripture. Pray that Jesus would shine on every page, and that the Spirit would fill their hearts with delight in the Savior.

DISCERNMENT

"The statutes of the LORD are trustworthy, making wise the simple" (v 7).

Our children encounter numerous decisions in their lives. Many times, it's difficult for them to know what to do. They'll be tempted to follow wrong paths or go along with the crowd. Pray that God would open your child's eyes to see the wisdom, understanding, and discernment given in his word.

TRUTH

"The decrees of the LORD are firm, and all of them are righteous" (v 9).

God's word never fades or goes out of fashion, no matter what our culture says to the contrary. His truth is firm. Pray that your child will receive this truth, and measure everything they hear and see against the straight and true guide of the Bible.

WARNING

"By them your servant is warned; in keeping them there is great reward" (v 11).

God's word not only gives wisdom; it offers warnings. It shows us how to live and how *not* to live. Pray that your child would "not merely listen to the word," but "do what it says" (James 1 v 22). As they heed God's warnings, pray that they also delight to realize that "in keeping [God's decrees] there is great reward." Ask God to bless your child as they trust and obey his word.

PRAYING THAT MY CHILD WILL...

LIVE IN HARMONY WITH OTHERS

TITUS 3 v 1-2

PRAYER POINTS:

_____

_____

_____

_____

Father, I pray that my children will live in community by...

SUBMITTING TO AUTHORITY

"Remind the people to be subject to rulers and authorities" (v 1).

Our homes are the first training ground for submission to authority. As a child learns to submit to a parent, it sets the stage for submitting to God's word. Pray that your child would be submissive to you, as well as to their teachers and other authorities.

OBEYING THE LAW

"... to be obedient" (v 1).

All children (and adults!) struggle to obey in certain areas. Consider your child: in what way is he or she specifically struggling to obey at the moment? Pray for your child, that the Lord will work in their heart and allow them to walk in joyful obedience in that area.

DOING GOOD TO OTHERS

"… to be ready to do whatever is good"
(v 1).

We not only want our children to obey—we hope they'll actively serve others. Ask God to give your children eyes to see those who are needy around them, and to enable them to be ready to do good to others.

 SPEAKING WITH KINDNESS

"… to slander no one, to be peaceable and
considerate" (v 2).

In our families, it's easy to develop habits like tattling and quarrelling with one another. Pray that your children would speak with kindness and respect toward others (especially their siblings!). Pray that your home will be marked by unity and peace rather than arguments and disputes.

 DISPLAYING COURTESY

"… always to be gentle toward everyone"
(v 2).

Praise God that every single life has value because each is made in his image. Pray that your child will treat all people—from the least to the greatest—with dignity, courtesy, and gentleness.

PRAYING THAT MY CHILD WILL...

BE WISE

PROVERBS 13 v 3-20

PRAYER POINTS:

_____

_____

_____

_____

Father, make my children wise with their...

 WORDS

> *"Those who guard their lips preserve their lives, but those who speak rashly will come to ruin" (v 3).*

Praise God that he freely gives wisdom to all who ask. It's especially needed with our words. Whether it's fighting between two siblings or an argument with a friend, rash words have power to harm. Pray that your child will be self-controlled with their words, as they speak to others, text, or communicate online.

 WORK

> *"A sluggard's appetite is never filled, but the desires of the diligent are fully satisfied" (v 4).*

How we go about our work matters. Children often want to hurry through chores, spending as little time on them as possible. Pray that the Lord would teach them the wisdom of being diligent in their labors, whether they are cleaning their room, sweeping the floor, or working on a project for school.

 **MONEY**

> *"Dishonest money dwindles away, but whoever gathers money little by little makes it grow" (v 11).*

"The love of money is a root of all kinds of evil" (1 Timothy 6 v 10). As teens begin to understand the power of money, it can lead them to make dishonest decisions or unwise choices. Pray that your child will make wise decisions and honor God with money.

 JUDGMENT

> *"Good judgment wins favor, but the way of the unfaithful leads to their destruction. All who are prudent act with knowledge, but fools expose their folly" (v 15-16).*

It takes time to learn good judgment. Pray that as you daily teach your children truth from error and right from wrong, the Lord will grow them in their understanding. As they grow, ask God to help them use their knowledge to make wise decisions.

 FRIENDSHIP

> *"Walk with the wise and become wise, for a companion of fools suffers harm" (v 20).*

When our children are young, we usually manage their friendships. As they age, they begin making their own choices about who they spend time with. Pray that your child will choose friends who are wise, and for godly mentors who will influence their choices for good.

PRAYING THAT MY CHILD WILL...

PRAYERFULLY SEEK GOD

MATTHEW 6 v 6-13

PRAYER POINTS:

_____

_____

_____

_____

Father, I pray that my child would offer prayers…

IN PRIVATE

> *"When you pray, go into your room, close
> the door and pray to your Father, who is
> unseen. Then your Father, who sees what
> is done in secret, will reward you"* (v 6).

So many things done in secret are wrong. However,
prayer is something we can do behind closed doors
that richly blesses the world around us. Pray that your
child may have a secret prayer life that yields a rich
reward from God.

HOPING FOR YOUR GLORY

> *"Our Father in heaven, hallowed be your
> name, your kingdom come, your will be
> done, on earth as it is in heaven"* (v 9-10).

Praise God that he reigns over all things in every way.
Ask God to allow your child to be one who seeks to
glorify the name of Jesus in all that they do, and that
this would be reflected in their prayers. May the Spirit
grow your child's desire to see God's will be done
and his kingdom come.

ASKING FOR DAILY BREAD

"Give us today our daily bread" (v 11).

It's easy to consider our own work and efforts as the source of what we need. One way to help our child understand God's provision is by teaching them to thank God at each mealtime. Pray that your child would be genuinely and increasingly thankful for all the ways God so richly provides for their needs: water to drink, food to eat, and shelter for rest.

SEEKING FORGIVENESS

"And forgive us our debts, as we also have forgiven our debtors" (v 12).

Each of us needs forgiveness, and each of us will have cause to forgive others. Pray that when your child sins, they will quickly turn to the Lord in confession and seek his forgiveness. Pray that they will remember their own need of forgiveness and freely forgive others who have hurt them.

FIGHTING TEMPTATION

"And lead us not into temptation, but deliver us from the evil one" (v 13).

When children are young, they may be tempted to snatch a toy from a friend or to throw a fit when they don't get their way. As they age, they may be tempted by materialism or sexual immorality. Pray today about the temptations they are facing. Ask the Lord to deliver them from evil as they prayerfully seek to battle sin.

THINGS TO PRAY

PRAYING THAT MY CHILD WILL...

BE CONTENT
IN ALL THINGS

PHILIPPIANS 4 v 4-13

PRAYER POINTS:

_____

_____

_____

_____

Father, may my children find their joy in you and…

REJOICE

> *"Rejoice in the Lord always. I will say it again: Rejoice!" (v 4).*

Spend some time praising God for who he is and all that he has done for you in Christ. Rejoice in the Lord! Then pray that your child will be a person who experiences great joy by worshiping and rejoicing in the Lord.

FIGHT ANXIETY

> *"Do not be anxious about anything, but in every situation, by prayer and petition, with thanksgiving, present your requests to God" (v 6).*

Anxiety quickly steals our joy. What is your child anxious about today? Whether it is a sports team they are hoping to make or an exam they are hoping to pass, pray they would experience the peace of God guarding their minds in Christ Jesus as they turn to him in prayer.

GUARD THEIR THOUGHTS

"Whatever is true, whatever is noble, whatever is right, whatever is pure, whatever is lovely, whatever is admirable—if anything is excellent or praiseworthy—think about such things" (v 8).

What we think about greatly affects our contentment. Our children often spend their mental energy comparing themselves to others or complaining about what they lack. Ask God to help them to take every thought captive to Christ and choose to think upon what is right, true, lovely, excellent, and praiseworthy.

 ### LEARN CONTENTMENT

"I have learned the secret of being content in any and every situation" (v 12).

Our children will experience times of plenty and times of want. The good news is that contentment is available in both. Pray that your child would learn the secret of contentment in every circumstance they face.

 ### TRUST JESUS

"I can do all this through him who gives me strength" (v 13).

Contentment is impossible in our own strength. We need a source of refreshment outside of ourselves. Consider where your child is struggling to be content. Pray they'll learn to depend on God's strength, not their own, as they seek to be content in all things.

PRAYING THAT MY CHILD WILL...

LOVE OTHERS

1 CORINTHIANS 13 v 4-5

PRAYER POINTS:

_____

_____

_____

_____

Father, I pray that your love will allow my child to love others...

 FREELY

"Love . . . does not envy" (v 4).

Praise God for the love he has poured out on each of us in Christ Jesus! When we envy someone else, it demonstrates that at some level we wrongly believe God has failed to be good to us. Pray that your child will understand the greatness of the gift God has given so that they can love others freely without envy.

 HUMBLY

"It does not boast" (v 4).

When we focus on ourselves, we boast to others about the accolades we have received. In what area is your child struggling with pride or boasting? Are you encouraging them toward pride or humility in their accomplishments? Pray that your child will focus not on what they have done but on what God has done.

3 RESPECTFULLY

"It does not dishonor others" (v 5).

It's painful to see our children hurt by the words and actions of others. It is just as difficult to see them dishonor others with their words and actions. Pray that your child will love others well by seeking to show them honor and encouragement.

4 SELFLESSLY

"It is not proud ... it is not self-seeking"
(v 4, 5).

From a young age, children tend to look out for themselves. If they see a toy they want, they take it. If someone gets in their way, they push them aside. Pray that your child will be able to put the needs of others before their own needs. Pray that, rather than be self-seeking in their behavior, they will be self-sacrificing.

5 GRACIOUSLY

"It is not easily angered, it keeps no record
of wrongs" (v 5).

It's amazing how long a track record siblings can keep of one another's offenses. Perhaps your children struggle with the comparison game called, "It's not fair!" Pray that the Lord would give your children a rich love for one another that isn't easily angered and shows grace instead of keeping score.

PRAYING THAT MY CHILD WILL...

STAND FIRM

EPHESIANS 6 v 10-17

PRAYER POINTS:

_____

_____

_____

_____

Father, I pray that my child will stand against the devil's schemes by putting on the full armor of God...

BELT OF TRUTH

"Stand firm then, with the belt of truth buckled around your waist" (v 14).

We know the devil prowls around like a roaring lion, looking for someone to devour (1 Peter 5 v 8). Pray that your child will remember the truth of God's word and stand firm against the devil's schemes.

BREASTPLATE OF RIGHTEOUSNESS

"... with the breastplate of righteousness in place, and with your feet fitted with the readiness that comes from the gospel of peace" (v 14-15).

Praise God that we are not dependent upon our own righteousness, but we have the perfect righteousness of Christ as our armor. Pray that your child will be ready to share this good news with someone in their life: a neighbor, a school friend, or a sport teammate.

SHIELD OF FAITH

"In addition to all this, take up the shield of faith, with which you can extinguish all the flaming arrows of the evil one" (v 16).

Faith in God acts as our shield against the enemy's flaming arrows. Jesus warned, "The thief comes only to steal and kill and destroy; I have come that they may have life, and have it to the full" (John 10 v 10). Pray that your child will know the full life found by faith in Jesus, and be protected from the enemy's attacks.

HELMET OF SALVATION

"Take the helmet of salvation" (v 17).

Our minds can often be the battleground of our faith. Sometimes, because we know we're not good enough for God, we falsely believe he won't save us. Satan spreads his lies so that we become fearful in our living. Pray that your child will guard their mind by remembering the free gift of God's salvation.

SWORD OF THE SPIRIT

"… and the sword of the Spirit, which is the word of God" (v 17).

While all the other parts of God's armor are defensive, the sword of the Spirit is our one weapon for attack. As we impress God's word on our children's hearts, we're preparing them for battle. Pray that your children will eagerly learn God's word so that his truth can help them battle against the lies of the enemy.

5 THINGS TO PRAY

PRAYING THAT I WILL...

SHARE THE GOODNESS OF GOD WITH MY CHILD

PSALM 78 v 1-7

PRAYER POINTS:

Lord, help me to be a parent who is faithful to…

 LISTEN

> *"My people, hear my teaching; listen to the words of my mouth" (v 1).*

Before we can tell our children about God, we need to listen to his teaching ourselves. In what ways are you seeking to know God through his word? Ask God to give you a listening heart that loves his truth.

 TELL

> *"We will tell the next generation the praise-worthy deeds of the LORD, his power, and the wonders he has done" (v 4).*

We tell our children so many things each day. How often do you remind them of all the wonders of God? In what ways could you help them to know of his glorious deeds? Spend a few moments now praising God for his goodness to you. Then pray that you would tell your children about the faithfulness of God each day—using even the ordinary moments of family life to point to Christ's extraordinary saving power.

3 TEACH

> *"He ... established the law in Israel, which he commanded our ancestors to teach their children" (v 5).*

We've been entrusted with our children and commanded to teach them God's word. In what ways are you teaching your children from the Bible? Pray that as you share God's word with your child, they will listen and learn.

4 TRUST

> *"Then they would put their trust in God" (v 7).*

Each day, as parents, we teach our children by our lives. As we set our hope in God, trusting in him through prayer, our children learn from our example. Perhaps today some worry weighs heavy on your heart—an illness, a financial concern, or a broken relationship. Pray that your heart will trust God in this hardship, and set an example for your family.

5 REMEMBER

> *"... and would not forget his deeds but would keep his commands" (v 7).*

As believers, we can look back in thankfulness as we remember the deeds of God—both in our own life and throughout history. Pray that the Lord would refresh and revive your heart for obedience to his commands as you remember his glorious works.

PRAYING THIS I WILL...

CREATE A HOME
OF PATIENCE
AND KINDNESS

COLOSSIANS 3 V 12-14

5 THINGS TO PRAY

PRAYING THAT I WILL...

CREATE A HOME OF PATIENCE AND KINDNESS

COLOSSIANS 3 v 12-14

PRAYER POINTS:

_____

_____

_____

_____

Father, by your grace, help me build a home that is...

 LOVING

> *"Therefore, as God's chosen people, holy and dearly loved..." (v 12).*

Praise God that in his rich mercy he chose you and saved you, and loves you dearly. One of the greatest gifts we can give our children is a home rich in love. Pray that your children will gain glimpses of God's love for them as they experience your love each day.

 COMPASSIONATE AND KIND

> *"Clothe yourselves with compassion [and] kindness" (v 12).*

Whether they are dealing with a bee sting or a broken heart, our children need compassion and kindness from us. Pray that as you remember God's kindness to you in Christ, you'll share that with your child.

3 HUMBLE

"… humility" (v 12).

As we parent, it's important to remember our daily need of God's forgiveness and mercy, so that we parent out of humility rather than pride. Where do you need God's grace today? Ask him for it. Then pray that the Lord would help your whole family to love one another with humility, seeking to serve rather than be served.

4 GENTLE AND PATIENT

"… gentleness and patience. Bear with each other" (v 12-13).

From the car to the couch or the dinner table—family members have to share their space! Our sin means we tend to rub each other the wrong way and cause frustration. Pray for each member of your family today, that you would treat each other with gentleness and patience, bearing with one another in grace and love.

5 FORGIVING

"Forgive one another if any of you has a grievance against someone. Forgive as the Lord forgave you" (v 13).

Every Christian is someone who has been forgiven much—praise God that your sin is never too far or too frequent to receive his forgiveness. Pray that you and your family will readily confess to one another other when you sin, and extend the same loving forgiveness.

PRAYING THAT I WILL...

TRUST THE LORD WITH MY CHILD

PSALM 27

PRAYER POINTS:

_____

_____

_____

_____

Father, help me as I parent to...

BE CONFIDENT IN YOU

"The LORD is my light and my salvation—
whom shall I fear?" (v 1).

Even with the abundance of parenting advice available, we often feel unsure and fearful as we make parenting decisions. Praise God that he is full of the wisdom we lack and provides light to illuminate our path. Ask him to give you a spirit of humble confidence in him for whatever you may fear today for your child.

SEEK YOU DAILY

"This only do I seek: that I may dwell in the
house of the LORD all the days of my life,
to gaze on the beauty of the LORD" (v 4).

Part of trusting the Lord with our children is remembering that our relationship with them is not the most important in our lives. While it's tempting to center our lives around our children's wants and schedules, the most important thing we can do is spend time with the Lord. Pray that you would seek him above all else.

3 SACRIFICE WITH JOY

"At his sacred tent I will sacrifice with shouts of joy" (v 6).

We're called to be "a living sacrifice" (Romans 12 v 1)—and parenthood certainly requires sacrifice. Most days, it's difficult to do so joyfully. Take a moment to confess the areas in which you're tempted to complain and grumble. Ask him to give you a heart of joy and worship as you sacrificially care for your family today, trusting that he sees every sacrifice and will use each one in his purposes for your family.

4 CALL TO YOU IN PRAYER

"Hear my voice when I call, LORD; be merciful to me and answer me" (v 7).

One of the greatest ways we entrust our children to the Lord is through our prayers. Consider each of your children. What concerns are on your heart? Call out to the Lord, asking him to be merciful to you as you parent.

5 TRUST YOUR TIMING

"Wait for the LORD; be strong and take heart and wait for the LORD" (v 14).

One of the hardest things to trust God with is your child's salvation. Perhaps you've been waiting for years for a sign of God's Spirit at work in them, or for a breakthrough in a particular area. Ask God to encourage your heart and help you to trust in his timing. Pray for strength to persevere in sharing Christ with your child and wrestling in prayer on their behalf.

PRAYING WHEN MY CHILD IS...

SUFFERING FROM DISAPPOINTMENT, LOSS, OR HURT

ROMANS 5 v 1-5

_____

_____

_____

_____

Father, when my child is suffering, allow them to...

GLORIFY YOUR NAME

"And we boast in the hope of the glory of God. Not only so, but we also glory in our sufferings" (v 2-3).

No parent wants to see their child suffer. Yet the Lord is able to work good from all the hurts they encounter: ear infections, painful gossip, learning difficulties, and unfair treatment. Ask God to glorify himself through your child's suffering as they fix their eyes on him.

ENDURE

"... because we know that suffering pro-duces perseverance" (v 3).

Our children may grow up to face difficult job situations, hard marriages, or unwanted illnesses. However old they are, our love for our children means that we hurt when they hurt. Pray that the Lord will use suffering in your child's life now to grow them in perseverance for the future; and that you would grow too as they grow.

GROW IN CHARACTER

"… perseverance [produces] character" (v 4).

Praise God that he never wastes an ounce of suffering. He promises to work all things for the good of conforming his people into the image of Jesus. Pray that, in their suffering, your child will reflect the character of Christ: "When he suffered, he made no threats. Instead, he entrusted himself to him who judges justly" (1 Peter 2 v 23).

HOPE

"… and character [produces] hope" (v 4).

Praise God that, in Christ, suffering doesn't end in bitterness or despair. It ends in hope. Pray that your child will be filled with hope in the midst of hardship, knowing that God walks with them in their grief and comforts them in their pain, and will one day wipe away every tear from their eyes.

REMEMBER

"God's love has been poured out into our hearts through the Holy Spirit" (v 5).

Our Father knows what it is to watch a beloved child suffer. "This is how God showed his love among us: He sent his one and only Son into the world that we might live through him" (1 John 4 v 9). God loves you so much that he allowed his Son to suffer in your place. Ask the Holy Spirit to comfort your heart and to bring healing and hope in your child's life today.

5 THINGS TO PRAY

PRAYING WHEN MY CHILD IS...

MAKING
FRIENDS

SELECTED PROVERBS

PRAYER POINTS:

_____

_____

_____

_____

Father, I pray that you would give my child friendships where they...

 ## CHOOSE WISELY

> *"The righteous choose their friends carefully"* (12 v 26).

Our children are easily influenced by those around them. Pray that the Lord would give your child wisdom from a young age to choose friends carefully. Pray also that he would provide friends who encourage them in faith and help them to make wise decisions.

 ## SPEAK CAREFULLY

> *"A perverse person stirs up conflict, and a gossip separates close friends"* (16 v 28).

The sting of gossip or unkind words is painful—especially in the teen years. Pray that your child will be careful with their words, using them to repair friendships and deepen relationships instead of tearing them apart. Pray that they would attract friends who speak with gentleness and compassion toward others.

LOVE CONSISTENTLY

"A friend loves at all times" (17 v 17).

Our children need more love than we can provide. Friends are an important part of God's good provision in their lives—thank God for them. Pray that the Lord will help your child to be a loving and loyal friend, who stands beside others in whatever circumstances they face.

 FOLLOW FAITHFULLY

"One who has unreliable friends soon comes to ruin, but there is a friend who sticks closer than a brother" (18 v 24).

Praise God that he does not leave us on our own but gives us the fellowship of other believers in the church. Pray that when your child grows up and leaves home, they will experience community within the church and find faithful friends who become like family.

 LIVE PEACEFULLY

"Do not make friends with a hot-tempered person, do not associate with one easily angered, or you may learn their ways and get yourself ensnared" (22 v 24-25).

Some relationships have the power to harm. Pray that your child will avoid friendships with those who may lead them astray. Ask the Lord to keep your child from hot-tempered friends and destructive anger.

PRAYING WHEN MY CHILD IS...

EXPERIENCING CHANGE, UNCERTAINTY, OR FEAR

JOSHUA 1 v 8-9

PRAYER POINTS:

_____

_____

_____

_____

Father, when my child is experiencing change, uncer-
tainty, or fear, let them...

 MEDITATE ON YOUR WORD

> *"Keep this Book of the Law always on your*
> *lips; meditate on it day and night" (v 8).*

Moving house or changing school can be difficult for
children. They tend to find security in routine. Pray
that wherever you go, God's word will be an anchor
and comfort for your family as you meditate on it day
and night.

 OBEY YOUR WORD

> *" ... so that you may be careful to do*
> *everything written in it" (v 8).*

Fear can so often lead to bad choices. When teenag-
ers are uncertain or fearful about their appearance,
friendships, or intelligence, they may be tempted to
dress inappropriately, follow the crowd, or cheat on a
test. Pray that your child will have a desire to do what
is right and obey God, even when they risk losing the
approval of others.

3 **PROSPER**

> *"Then you will be prosperous and successful" (v 8).*

So many of our own fears revolve around our child's future. Will they get a good job if they don't get the best grades? What if I can't help them financially? Will this upheaval scar them for life? Pray that in the future, God would provide your child with all the prosperity and success they need for their spiritual good—no more and no less (Proverbs 30 v 8-9).

4 **BE STRONG AND COURAGEOUS**

> *"Be strong and courageous. Do not be afraid; do not be discouraged" (v 9).*

When children are afraid, the most natural thing for them is to cover their eyes and shrink back in fear—as they get older, their responses may look different, but the instinct is the same. What is your child currently facing that is causing them anxiety? Pray that they will have strength and courage to face those fears today.

5 **BE SURE OF YOUR PRESENCE**

> *"The LORD your God will be with you wherever you go" (v 9).*

Praise God that he will be with your child wherever they go. While we are limited and cannot be everywhere at once, God is everywhere, and he neither slumbers nor sleeps. Pray that your child will experience the security of God's presence in the midst of change and uncertainty.

PRAYING WHEN MY CHILD IS...

LONELY

PSALM 16

PRAYER POINTS:

_____

_____

_____

_____

Father, when my child is lonely, help them to...

TAKE REFUGE IN YOU

"Keep me safe, my God, for in you I take refuge. I say to the LORD, 'You are my Lord; apart from you I have no good thing'" (v 1).

There are so many reasons why our children can feel lonely. Perhaps they are going off to school or summer camp for the first time, and they don't know anyone. Or maybe they have a large group of friends but still feel isolated or different from everyone else. Pray that your child will turn to God in their loneliness, taking refuge in him and remembering his goodness.

FIND FELLOWSHIP

"I say of the holy people who are in the land, 'They are the noble ones in whom is all my delight'" (v 3).

Praise God that he cares about our loneliness and has given us a spiritual family in the church. Pray that your child will find fellowship with other believers from the church who will ease the loneliness they feel.

AVOID FALSE FRIENDS

> *"Those who run after other gods will suffer more and more. I will not pour out libations of blood to such gods or take up their names on my lips" (v 4).*

When children feel lonely, they can be tempted to follow the crowd in an attempt to belong. Pray that your child will have the resolve to not walk in the ways of those who live in opposition to God.

 SEEK YOUR COUNSEL

> *"I will praise the LORD, who counsels me; even at night my heart instructs me" (v 7).*

Pray that your child will be able to praise the Lord in the midst of their loneliness, giving thanks for his counsel. Pray that as they seek God in their loneliness, they will find comfort, wisdom, and direction.

 REJOICE IN YOUR PRESENCE

> *"You make known to me the path of life; you will fill me with joy in your presence, with eternal pleasures at your right hand" (v 11).*

There is an eternal source of joy offered to us in the Lord's presence. At times, loneliness allows an opportunity for our children to draw near to Christ and experience abundant life in him in new ways. Pray that your child will follow the path of life, looking first to God to satisfy their relational needs.

PRAYING WHEN MY CHILD IS...

MAKING A DIFFICULT DECISION

PHILIPPIANS 1 v 9-11

PRAYER POINTS:

_____

_____

_____

_____

Father, as my child wrestles with a difficult decision, help them to...

 PRAY

"*And this is my prayer*" (v 9).

When our older children and teens make decisions, they often turn quickly to human wisdom and advice. Pray that your child will begin with prayer, seeking God's help first as they make important decisions in life.

 LOVE YOUR WAYS

"*... that your love may abound more and more*" (v 9).

Discernment is rooted in relationship with God. Pray that your child would develop a deep love for God that grows with each passing year—and that loving him and loving others would be their main motive when making decisions. Pray for your child to also have an affection for God's word: "Open my eyes that I may see wonderful things in your law" (Psalm 119 v 18).

BE FILLED WITH INSIGHT

"… in knowledge and depth of insight" (v 9).

Ask God to fill your child with understanding and knowledge—of their own strengths and weaknesses, of other people, and chiefly, of God himself. Pray that as they memorize verses, read Bible stories, and sing worship songs, they will grow in depth of insight, gaining wisdom to guide them for years to come.

 ## DISCERN WHAT IS BEST

"… so that you may be able to discern what is best and may be pure and blameless for the day of Christ" (v 10).

Our children will have so many important decisions to make throughout their lives. Ask God to give your child wisdom beyond their years to be able to discern what is best—both in how to live and what to believe. Pray that your child would make decisions with an eternal perspective, as they fix their eyes on Christ's return.

 ## GLORIFY YOU

"… filled with the fruit of righteousness that comes through Jesus Christ—to the glory and praise of God" (v 11).

Praise God that he fills his children with righteousness through Jesus Christ! Ask God to fill your child with a deep desire to live a life of worship, glorifying God in all things. Pray that your child will honor God with the choices they make.

PRAYING WHEN MY CHILD IS...

GROWN UP

JEREMIAH 29 v 11-13

PRAYER POINTS:

_____

_____

_____

_____

Father, I pray for my child in the future, that when they are grown up, you would give them…

 ETERNAL PROSPERITY

"*'For I know the plans I have for you,'
declares the LORD, 'plans to prosper
you'*" *(v 11).*

Praise God that he knows the plans he has for our children. Their lives are not random; rather, "all the days ordained for [them] were written in [God's] book before one of them came to be" (Psalm 139 v 16). Pray that the Lord will prosper your child with eternal riches: faith, hope, and love.

 ETERNAL PROTECTION

"*… and not to harm you*" *(v 11).*

It's easy to worry about the future world our children will inherit. Commit these fears to the Lord, and ask him to protect your children, both physically and spiritually. Pray that God will keep them from all harm and lead them in paths of righteousness.

3 A HOPE-FILLED HOME

"... plans to give you hope" (v 11).

Much of our children's future will be impacted by whether or who they marry. Pray that, if your child marries, their spouse will love the Lord, be faithful and hard-working, open their home in hospitality to those who are lonely, and help your child to hope in Christ. Whether they are married or single, pray that their home would be a place of grace and goodness, where the hope of the gospel is proclaimed.

 4 A FUTURE OF BLESSING

"... and a future" (v 11).

Pray for the generations of children that may come from your family. Ask that, if granted, future grandchildren and great-grandchildren may love the Lord and walk by the Spirit. Pray that they may be richly blessed and be a blessing to many.

 5 A RELATIONSHIP WITH CHRIST

"Then you will call on me and come and pray to me, and I will listen to you. You will seek me and find me when you seek me with all your heart" (v 12-13).

More than anything else, the thing we hope for our children is that they walk in relationship with Jesus. Pray that in the future your child will call out to the Lord, listen to him, and seek him all their days. Praise God that he hears the cries of all who call on his name!

EXPLORE THE WHOLE SERIES

"A THOUGHT-PROVOKING, VISION-EXPANDING, PRAYER-STIMULATING TOOL. SIMPLE, BUT BRILLIANT."
SINCLAIR FERGUSON

thegoodbook.co.uk | .com

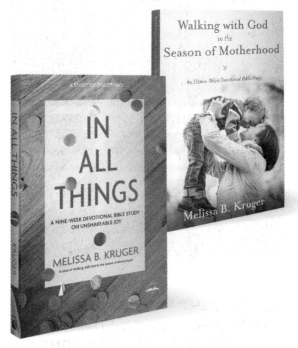

thegoodbook
COMPANY

BIBLICAL | RELEVANT | ACCESSIBLE

At The Good Book Company, we are dedicated to helping Christians and local churches grow. We believe that God's growth process always starts with hearing clearly what he has said to us through his timeless word—the Bible.

Ever since we opened our doors in 1991, we have been striving to produce Bible-based resources that bring glory to God. We have grown to become an international provider of user-friendly resources to the Christian community, with believers of all backgrounds and denominations using our books, Bible studies, devotionals, evangelistic resources, and DVD-based courses.

We want to equip ordinary Christians to live for Christ day by day, and churches to grow in their knowledge of God, their love for one another, and the effectiveness of their outreach.

Call us for a discussion of your needs or visit one of our local websites for more information on the resources and services we provide.

Your friends at The Good Book Company

thegoodbook.com | thegoodbook.co.uk
thegoodbook.com.au | thegoodbook.co.nz
thegoodbook.co.in